Beyond the Horizon
With the cat & the tortoise
Black and White Edition

Beyond the Horizon

With the cat & the tortoise

Black and White Edition

"I wonder what lies beyond the horizon?" Said the cat.

"The unknown." Replied the tortoise.

"I would like to see the unknown."
Said the cat.

"I would like to stay at home."
Said the tortoise.

"But wouldn't you like to see where
an adventure would lead?"
Asked the cat.

"I'm too small for an adventure!"
Replied the tortoise.

"I heard the most wonderful
things happen during adventures."
Said the cat.
"If only we were brave enough to
take the first step."

"But I'm not brave enough..."
said the tortoise,

"... and I take very small steps!"

"Bravery comes in all sizes."
Said the cat.

"It isn't the size of your
stride that matters...
but the size of your
heart."

"That made you smile, didn't it?"
Said the cat.

"I like to smile."
Said the tortoise.

"So do I." Replied the cat.

And so...
their adventure begins.

What lies...
Beyond the Horizon?

"It's too foggy to see where we're going!" Said the tortoise.

"That happens sometimes..."
replied the cat.

"... but if we wait long enough
for it to lift, a bright new
world will be revealed."

"That's better," said the tortoise.
"I can see now."

"So can I." Replied the cat.

"The horizon seems like such a long way." Said the tortoise.

"Yes, it does." Replied the cat. "But we should focus on the journey, rather than the length of the road."

"I'm starting to get rather chilly now."
Said the tortoise.

"I don't mind the cold." Replied the cat.

"I like it better in the sun," said the tortoise, "I don't like change."

"But not all change is bad," replied the cat, "without winter there would be no spring... and without spring there would be no flowers."

"I like flowers." Said the tortoise.

"So do I." Replied the cat

"I feel rather hungry now." Said the tortoise.

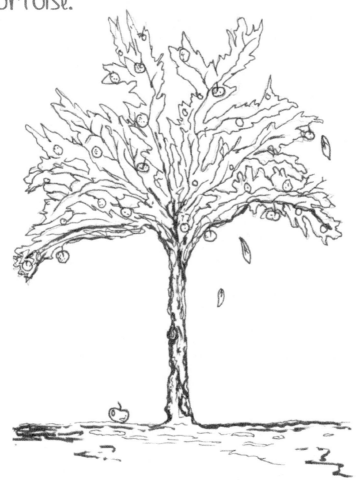

"Look, I see an apple tree." Replied the cat.

"That tree is far too tall for me," said the tortoise, "can I climb on your back?"

"Of course," replied the cat, "sometimes apples are out of reach, until we ask for help."

"That's much better." Said the tortoise.

"I don't like apples," replied the cat, "I prefer mice!"

"Everyone likes different things," said the tortoise, "it would be awfully boring if we were all the same."

"Will you always be my friend?" Asked the tortoise.

"I don't see why not," replied the cat, "as long as we stick together, nothing can pull us apart."

"Do you think we will ever reach the horizon?" Asked the tortoise.

"I think we might." Replied the cat.

"But you sound very uncertain."
Said the tortoise.

"I am," replied the cat, "but with
an uncertain future... comes
infinite possibilities."

"I feel very tired, now."
Said the cat.

"So do I." Said the tortoise.

And so...
           they slept.

"It's time to wake up." Said the tortoise.

"But I'm still very tired." Replied the cat.

"The bravest thing a tired mind can do... is wake up." Said the tortoise.

"I feel very thirsty after all that sleep." Said the cat.

"Let's try and find some water." Replied the tortoise.

"But where are we going to find water out here?" Asked the cat.

"We must dig!" Replied the tortoise.

And so...

they dug.

"How far should we dig?"
Asked the cat.

"The deeper we dig, the more we'll

discover." Replied the tortoise.

"I think I've found some," said the cat, "but it's only a ripple!"

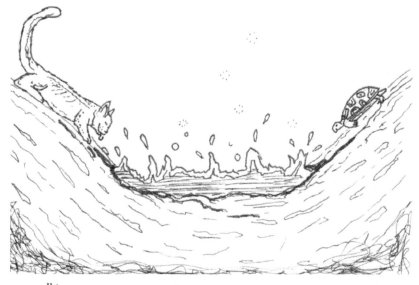

"But a ripple in a stream, can lead to waves in an ocean."
Replied the tortoise.

"Here," said the cat,
"you can have the first drink."

"Oh, what a thoughtful gift."
Replied the tortoise.

"It's not a gift," said the cat,
"I'm just being kind."

"But not all gifts have bows,"
replied the tortoise,
"some come wrapped in love."

"Oh dear... I think I'm stuck in this hole," said the tortoise, "will you help me?"

"Of course." Replied the cat.

"I don't like asking for help,"
said the tortoise, "I'm not
usually brave enough."

"But sometimes, asking for help
is the bravest thing you can
do." Replied the cat.

"I don't like to talk much, either."
Said the tortoise.

"Why not?" Asked the cat.

"Because I'm not very clever."
Replied the tortoise.

"But the ability to talk does not make you wise," said the cat, "it's the ability to listen... and you are the wisest friend I have."

"Do you think following the horizon will make us happy?" Asked the tortoise.

"I do." Replied the cat.

"Why?" Asked the tortoise.
"Because those who
follow their own
horizons, are usually the
ones who find happiness."
Said the cat.

And so...
they journeyed onward.

"Oh look, I see a beaver."
Said the cat.

"So do I."
Replied the tortoise.

"What are you doing?"
Asked the cat.

"I'm building a bridge."
Replied the beaver.

"Why?" Asked the cat.

"So that I can reach the other side." Replied the beaver.

"You look awfully tired," said the tortoise, "why don't you finish it tomorrow?"

"Because what happens tomorrow, is determined by what we do today." Replied the beaver.

"Would you like some help?"
Asked the cat.

"I certainly would." Replied the beaver.

And so...
they helped.

"Thank you for your help,"
said the beaver, "now I can
finally reach the other side."

"You're welcome," replied the cat,
"all we gave you was our time."

"Giving someone your time, is often the greatest gift you can give." Replied the beaver.

"Here, I want you to have this bucket." Said the beaver.

"Why?" Replied the cat.

"There's a stream over there,"
said the beaver,
"you can fill it with water."

"Thank you," replied the cat,
"and goodbye."

"Goodbye." Said the tortoise.

"Goodbye." Said the beaver.

And so...
they went to the stream.

"It's an awfully slow stream," said the cat, "It's going to take forever to fill this bucket."

"It may only be filling one drop at a time," replied the tortoise, "but at least it's still filling."

And so...
their adventure continued.

Across the beaver's bridge, to the other side.

"We're getting closer to the horizon." Said the cat.

"We've come a long way."
Replied the tortoise.

"And to think you said you
weren't brave." Said the cat.

"I'm braver than I thought."
Replied the tortoise.

"Oh dear, look at that crooked tree," said the cat, "it is a shame to see things broken."

"Even the mightiest trees can be broken by the wind," replied the tortoise, "but being broken doesn't mean it's the end."

"Look up there on that branch," said the tortoise, "there's a family of birds using that crooked tree as their home."

"Oh yes, I see them." Replied the cat.

"Even something broken can be beautiful." Said the tortoise.

"I do wish I could hear them singing."
Said the cat.

"We should be quiet for a moment."
Replied the tortoise.

"Why?" Asked the cat.

"Because we will only hear them
sing, once we've silenced our
minds." Said the tortoise.

"But we won't reach the horizon
if we take a moment for
ourselves." Said the cat.

"There is always time to take
a moment for ourselves."
Replied the tortoise.

"We have been sitting for so long," said the cat, "that it's getting awfully dark again."

"It certainly is." Replied the tortoise.

"I think it's going to be a long night." Said the cat.

"Then I think we should sleep," replied the tortoise, "for the night is only long to those who stay awake."

And so...
they slept.

Early next morning...

"Do you think it was a good idea to seek the horizon?" Asked the cat. "Perhaps I should have stayed at home, too."

"I think it was an excellent idea!" Replied the tortoise. "In order for anything good to happen... an idea must become an action."

"There are so many beautiful flowers out here." Said the cat.

"I think we should sit with them." Replied the tortoise.

"I've never sat with a flower before."
Said the cat.

"Only by taking the time to sit with a
flower, can we truly appreciate their
beauty." Replied the tortoise.

"There's a yummy mouse hiding in these flowers," said the cat, "yes, very yummy indeed."

"I don't think you should
hold him like that." Replied
the tortoise.

"Why not?" Asked the cat.
"Because holding a mouse by its tail,
is like holding onto anger. The only
way to ease the struggle, is by
letting it go."

And so...
the cat dropped the mouse.

"Oh look, its family have come to join us." Said the tortoise.

"I didn't know mice had families." Replied the cat.

"Nothing ever exists entirely on its own." Said the tortoise.

"I'm sorry I almost ate you, little mouse." Said the cat.

"That's quite alright," replied the mouse, "I've never been eaten before."

"You saved that little mouse."
Said the tortoise.

"It was the least I could do."
Said the cat.

"One moment is all it takes to change a life." Replied the tortoise.

"I think we're halfway there," said the cat, "I can see the horizon."

"And I can see how far we've come." Replied the tortoise.

"My stomach is rumbling, now,"
said the cat, "I feel very hungry."

"I still have a slice of apple if
you'd like it." Replied the tortoise.
"Perhaps I will,"
said the cat, "it's
always nice to try
new things."

"That was actually very nice," said the cat, "but it was all you had."

"I like to give," replied the tortoise, "even when I only have a little."

"How many days have we
been walking?" Asked the cat.

"I don't know," replied the
tortoise, "I like to live one day
at a time."

"Oh dear, I think it's starting to rain." Said the cat.

"I think the best thing to do when it starts to rain," replied the tortoise, "is let it rain."

"I think we'll need to use this branch
to cross the river." Said the cat.

"But I don't think I can," replied the
tortoise, "it's an awfully long way."

"But you never know what you can achieve until you try." Said the cat.

And so...
they crossed the river.

"I don't want to let go of this branch," said the tortoise, "I'd feel much safer if I stayed here."

"But we should always let
go of the things that
are holding us back."
Replied the cat.

"There... that wasn't difficult,
was it?" Said the cat.

"Things rarely are as bad as they
seem." Replied the tortoise.

"I can see a mountain."

Said the tortoise.

"Me too," replied the cat, "I think
we're almost at the horizon."

"I don't think I can climb a mountain." Said the tortoise.

"And I didn't think I liked apples." Replied the cat.

"It's an awfully tall mountain," said the tortoise, "I feel like giving up."

"Will you?" Asked the cat.

"I don't think so." Replied the tortoise.

"That's good," said the cat, "because the only way to reach the horizon, is by carrying on, even when we feel like giving up."

"Do you miss home?"
Asked the
cat.

"No," replied the tortoise, "I'm far
too busy concentrating on the
present."

"I think we're almost at the top."
Said the cat.

"All because we took that first
step." Replied the tortoise.

"I'm glad I came with you."
Said the tortoise.

"And I'm glad you came with me."
Replied the cat.

"Oh, hello little butterfly," said
the tortoise, "you make this
look very easy."

"I've had lots of practice."
Replied the butterfly.

"But flying looks easier than climbing." Said the cat.

"Only because you've never flown." Replied the butterfly.

"I can't wait to see beyond the horizon." Said the cat.

"Neither can I."
Replied the tortoise.

And so...
they continued to climb.

"Isn't the world beautiful?" Said
the cat. "I never realised,
until now."

"It's often the most obvious
things we miss." Replied
the tortoise.

At the peak of the mountain
they look,
Beyond the Horizon.

"I think we've finally made it."
Said the cat.

"I think so too."
Replied the tortoise.

"Now that we're here, I feel quite sad." Said the cat.

"Why is that?" Asked the tortoise.

"Because the journey is often better than the destination." Replied the cat.

"The world is truly beautiful from up here." Said the cat.

"The world is beautiful from down there too." Replied the tortoise

"You can see your home from here." Said the cat.

"Where?" Asked the tortoise.

"Just beyond the horizon." Replied the cat.

"Would you like to go home, now?" Asked the cat.

"As long as we're together... we're always home." Replied the tortoise.

And so...
their story continues...

Thank you for coming on this journey. For many years now I have created books which focus on mindfulness and the here and now. I wanted to try something a little different with this book, by creating a story and building a narrative around some valuable life lessons that we can all benefit from.

I hope you have enjoyed going on this adventure with the cat and the tortoise. These characters were inspired by my two pets, Mitsy and Perri: The real-life cat and tortoise, who fill my days with happiness.

All the best,
Chris.

Mitsy

Perri

About the Author

Christopher Stokes was born in an English town called Walsall. He has been fortunate enough to see some of his books become bestsellers in various Amazon categories, and with the constant support of his family, he has written novels, novellas and numerous short stories.
He also turned his passion for art into a plethora of illustrated children's stories, alongside a popular series of colouring books.

You can find him on Facebook at:
Christopher Mark Stokes' World of Colour.

Printed in Great Britain
by Amazon

21095923R00061